MAN IN ESSENCE

Folk Tales and Photographs
from
IRIAN JAYA, INDONESIA

Folk tales collected and photographs taken by
LAURENS HILLHOUSE

Edited and introduced by
MARIE V. MOHR-GRANDSTAFF

Folk tales were translated by Marie V. Mohr-Grandstaff.

Sketches were selected from the handwritten journals
of Laurens Hillhouse.

Library of Congress Catalog Card Number: 90-83582

ISBN: 0-9627359-0-6

Printed and bound in the United States of America

We dedicate this book to the memory of our son, Larry, and to his "brothers and sisters in the great race of humans" — the indigenous people of Irian Jaya — among whom he lived for a time, and whose native culture and lifestyle he appreciated and respected.

Jim and Marion Hillhouse

CONTENTS

INTRODUCTION

       Laurens Hillhouse, known to his family as Larry, to his college classmates as Lars, and to his friends throughout the South Pacific as Tony, was born January 25, 1946 in Palo Alto, California. His early education was in Palo Alto and later he went to Salem, Oregon to attend Willamette University. He studied psychology and graduated in 1967. In the fall of that year he joined the Peace Corps and served for two and one-half years in Western Samoa. Being a person who was always eager to learn and explore, Larry continued his journey to other parts of the South Pacific and on to South East Asia for six more years. Thailand, Malaysia, Cambodia, Singapore and numerous islands in Indonesia were some of the many places that he visited.

The island and the people of Irian Jaya (West New Guinea), captured his attention in a unique manner. He lived with the highland and valley tribes of this region for approximately eighteen months.

Upon Larry's return to the United States in 1976, he carried out various projects attempting to translate these valuable experiences into tangible forms, hoping to share and bring to others some of the riches and knowledge he had gained. He arranged exhibitions consisting of black and white photos of the aboriginal people of Irian, ethnic art objects, carved war shields, ancestor figures, bowls, masks, weapons and ornaments, original music from Irian taped on location and color slide presentations. The M. H. deYoung Memorial Museum and the California Academy of Sciences, San Francisco; the Lowie Museum of Anthropology at the University of California, Berkeley; California State University, Hayward; and the University of California, Santa Cruz, have held exhibitions of his materials in their halls. Larry called these programs MAN IN ESSENCE and that is the source from which the title for this book has come. A permanent collection of Larry's artifacts is at the deYoung Museum in San Francisco, California.

Larry's earth journey was interrupted abruptly on June 21, 1978, after a long, painful and most courageous struggle against cancer. "That strong amazing spirit broke free at last from the confines of his body which had grown too weak to contain it any longer and now journeys on in other realms," said a close friend of his shortly after his untimely death. Many hopes and dreams of his were not yet realized. The efforts in this book represent a desire to see at least some of his wishes fulfilled.

In addition to photos and artifacts, Larry also collected many folk tales from Irian. My acquaintance with this remarkable young man came about because of these stories. He contacted me to assist him in transcribing and translating these legends. At that time he spoke enthusiastically about his plans to publish the stories and use some of his photos to illustrate them. In the spring of 1978 we said farewell as we departed on our respective journeys, he to Hawaii for a rest and I to Indonesia for research. His parting words still echo in my heart, "Do drop by when you return, perhaps I will have more translation work for you."

Some months later when I returned to California I went to his home and learned from his mother that he had died while I was away. After many discussions, Larry's parents and I decided to continue his project.

MAN IN ESSENCE is an attempt to reproduce as closely as possible Larry's concept of combining photograph and legend from aboriginal Irian.

The following is a brief introduction Larry gave when presenting one of his exhibits which included music and legends.

* * *

"Through the portraits and stories of Asmat men, women and children, it is hoped that these people may come alive and be understood as the personalities that they are—brothers and sisters—in the great race of humans. They live in a vast primordial swamp land where the earth remains in its infancy. Life must be armored and cunning to survive in this primal environment. Incredibly, people live here. They are food gatherers, fishers, ritual headhunters, master oarsmen, superb sculptors of wood, drummers, story tellers, believers in the power of ancestor spirits.

"Until the present generation of adults they have lived naturally, as an element of their jungle surroundings, without the dubious benefits of the 'advanced' world.

"The Asmat and all of Irian is now claimed by the Indonesian government. Christian missionaries are panning for souls; oil companies invade with helicopters and food in tin cans. The people of Irian are experiencing the effects of guns, gospel and goods. The ethnic virginity of the Asmat is forever lost. The people who are at home in the dawning of the world must now absorb and understand in one lifetime, half a million years of human technological evolution—or perish!"

Share the experience of primary man
who lives within the whole
turning with the cycles of nature
who makes only the first interruptions
causing only the slightest imbalances

learn his laws of survival

meet minds behind painted faces

follow the ballet of his movement

sing his songs

glimpse his essence
before he is lost in the contagious rot of civilization
and discovers that he is "primitive"

                    Laurens Hillhouse
                    Jakarta, 1975

Laurens Hillhouse in village with friends

The oral tradition, prevalent among non-literate groups of people, is a living art form. The story teller is usually an older person held in esteem and frequently has some kind of authority in the village. The stories retain their general pattern from generation to generation; however, the narrator colors them with his own interpretation. Larry recounts an experience in a village where he was present for such an occasion.

* * *

"The typewritten page cannot communicate the atmosphere or excitement of the story telling in the middle of a moonlit night in a riverside village in the jungle swamps of the Asmat. The night is bright enough for people to be outside (when there is no moon the village is deathly still). The tide water is quite high, flooding the little creeks and marshes of the village. Various palms are silhouetted against the sky, insects and frogs are chirping and burping and some birds are calling. The gathering of people is spontaneous and they are of mixed age. As the story teller continues the story, people participate by cheering, laughing, silence, groaning, suggesting words, repeating phrases, imitating gestures, chanting refrains, etc.

"The story teller is so dramatic that you have a hard time not understanding the story even if you don't know the language. The general topic is sufficient. He uses his arms to point, his body to make sound effects (e.g., beating on his fists to imitate drums), his posture to enact the action. If the story relates waiting in an ambush, he crouches low, whispers, orders imaginary people behind him to be quiet, creeps around like a snake, etc.

"The listeners are silent in anticipation of the attack! When the canoes in the story approach he gives the signal and screams the attack. His body becomes rigid and threatening as he kills and collects the dead enemy. He portrays the cutting off of the head, the slicing of arms and legs, all with the excited flush of victory. As the triumphant canoes approach the village jubilant and victorious, he acts out the excitement of the women with their shouts of joy and dancing as the enemy bodies are carried to the *jeu*, the heads being held in triumph.

All during this he switches roles from victor to enemy, showing them cringing in fear and weeping in defeat. Throughout the entire story the crowd supports the narration with cheering, laughing, mocking, jeering and silence. Other men who know the story or remember the event prompt him on details, correct mistakes and add embellishments."

* * *

There are legends that reflect the power of the spirits. Most natural phenomena have explanatory legends. Punishment of the evil-doer, the Old Testament tradition of an eye for an eye and a tooth for a tooth, also known as the "pay back system," is the usual story line. The conclusion is often bizarre and unexpected. Magic and sorcery and ancestral spirits are also dominant themes.

One final quote from Larry's journal before we read the stories and legends of the people of Irian.

* * *

"The afternoon closes in on one of those psychedelic lowland sunsets. I think of the mountains of Irian, of New Guinea, reflecting that I have probably climbed and descended the last one. It fills me with a kind of sadness and respect, leaving behind this majestic, hellish, primally beautiful country which I have worshiped and cursed. The Star Mountains, snow capped, stand proudly in the distance, monumental, nearly forever; from these heights I am descending."

* * *

Larry has descended from the heights of these magnificent mountains and regions of Irian and ascended now to heights we know not. My hope is that whatever realm that may be, he now looks on kindly with approval and respect at the fruits of his sojourns which are presented here. I am honored and pleased to be the instrument of this offering. Through the portraits and stories of these people, may they "come alive and be understood as the personalities that they are—brothers and sisters—in the great race of humans."

Marie V. Mohr-Grandstaff

THE CREATION OF
LAKE ASBOLD

Hidden high in the cloud-shrouded cordillera of Central Irian lies an isolated lake. However, it was not always a lake. The people of Bokondini tell of the time it was a fertile valley where their ancestors built their beehive-shaped houses and cultivated their yam gardens. Unkindness toward a lowly mongrel dog seems to have brought about the end of this valley community.

It was pig feast time for the inhabitants of the valley. Scores of people lined the bank of the Kambo River. They were washing the entrails of the many pigs that had been slaughtered. A mangy, starving dog meekly approached the first person and begged for a small scrap of intestine to ease his gnawing hunger. The person refused with a

curse, as did the next one and the next one and so on down the line. The people not only refused him a scrap of food, but kicked him and threw stones in order to drive him away. Still, the poor scrawny creature begged, hoping to find someone with a kind heart.

After many rebuffs, the outcast dog humbly approached the last person on the river bank. It was an old woman whose face showed signs that she herself had suffered some hard times. With his tail between his legs and his body tense prepared for the pain of another stone or kick, the dog begged for a morsel of meat. Pity filled the woman when she saw what the poor dog had already suffered. She offered the dog some pieces of meat with the same sympathy a mother might show to her own child. As he ate he forgot his pains and aches and he was filled with gratitude toward the woman.

That night when she returned home she allowed the mangy dog to follow her and decided to keep him and always feed him so that he would never have to be hungry again. When they reached the house she was astonished when the dog began to speak to her. He said, "In a few days a heavy downpour will begin and it will cause the Mabiyogup River to flood. In order to be safe you must take your family and all your possessions and go high up on Mount Biambaga."

She quickly went and told her husband what the dog had said, but he didn't believe it. Instead, he was furious with her for having brought home the scrawny, mangy animal. Nevertheless, the woman took her small son and their most important possessions and found a safe place high up on the mountain.

Then the sky opened with a deluge such as the valley had never before experienced. The flood waters surged over the huts so quickly that no one had time to escape. The kindly woman, her son and a humble dog that talked were the only survivors of that community that had once been so prosperous. When you go there now all you will see are the clear, cool, sparkling waters of Lake Asbold.

"SAIL EARS"
—THE GIANT OF ARGUNI

The two brothers of the family Taruna, Kotisamemba and Mimau, were expert fishermen and pig hunters. One day they paddled their canoe far out in Bintuni Bay to try for the biggest fish. Before they had made a single catch, a huge whale rose up from the depths and swallowed them, canoe and all. Inside the belly of the whale they pondered their situation and plotted a plan which might help them escape. They built a fire and began cutting off pieces of the whale's intestines, which they roasted and ate. They ate and ate for several days, cutting their way up through the stomach into the chest cavity. When they cut into its heart, the whale died, throwing itself upon the shore of Bantunisa. From inside the enormous body, Kotisamemba and Mimau heard the sounds of the waves breaking on

the shore. They bored a hold in the side of the whale and stepped out
into the afternoon sunlight.

The two brothers did not recognize the shore. It was all new
and strange land to them. They started walking toward a column of
smoke rising above the trees to the east. Having walked a good
distance, they came to a village called Odarewar. There was a house
standing on stilts, set apart from the rest of the village. They approached it and boldly climbed up the notched log which led into the
doorway. Inside they met an old woman who lived alone. Her name
was Soma. She welcomed Kotisamemba and Mimau like sons. The
two brothers settled there with Soma and made this their new home.

One day after their arrival in Odarewar, Kotisamemba and
Mimau went into the jungle to hunt wild boar. Their skill paid off as
usual and they returned with a fat young pig, big enough to feed the
three of them for several days. They cleaned the pig and threw the
insides in the water to drift away. Those drifting pig entrails started a
round of trouble for the two brothers.

The entrails drifted far across the bay, landing on the coast of
Arguni Island. A giant lived there. He had wild black hair and an
enormous pair of floppy ears. He had a voracious appetite and a mean
disposition. Arguni was always victorious in raids and warfare
because of the giant. He was called Tingararae, which means "Sail
Ears."

Tingararae happened to be line fishing just at the spot where
the pig entrails were. He saw the guts and said to himself, "*Ahe-o!*
Somebody is preparing pig meat!" He looked at the horizon and saw
smoke rising on the mainland across the bay. That was all the greedy
giant needed to arouse him to action. He pushed his canoe off from
shore. Gripping both ears with his hands, he raised the great auditory
flaps into the wind and sailed swiftly across the sea. Following the
column of smoke, he reached the house where the pig meat was being
cooked. The old woman, Soma, was home alone tending the fire.
Tingararae picked up the iron tongs and lifted Soma up by the neck
like a snared lizard, then tossed her out of the house into the mud

below. He devoured half of the pig, stuffed the remainder in his bag, returned to the canoe, raised his billowy ears, and sailed back quickly to Arguni.

The two brothers returned to find the old woman alone in the house with no pig meat. "Mama," they asked bewildered, "how is it possible that you could eat one whole pig in the time we were gone?"

She told them about the giant of Arguni, his big ears and monstrous appetite. They sat there wide-eyed, holding their breath, as she told her incredible tale. Finally Kotisamemba spoke, "We must stand watch next time to find out if this is really true. Then we will decide what to do."

The following afternoon the brothers caught another wild pig. Before starting the cooking fire, they decided that Mimau would hide inside the house while Kotisamemba watched from a hiding place at the edge of the jungle. Sure enough, shortly after the smoke from the fire began to rise, a peculiar double-sailed craft appeared far out on the horizon. It was coming closer at high speed. Soon Kotisamemba saw the weirdest sight he had ever seen. A gigantic hairy man, perched on a narrow canoe, was sailing across the bay holding aloft his two immense ears, like the sky goddess hanging out clouds in the wind. He came to shore, entered the house and threw Mama Soma to the ground. Then he took all the pig meat and hoisted his ears for the return sail to his island.

"It's true brother!" cried Mimau when they met at the house. "That giant took all the meat. He would have killed me. I was trembling with fear!"

"But he is a man, not a spirit," reasoned Kotisamemba, "we can take care of him."

The next day they asked Mama Soma to build a fire. They put the points of their spears in the flames until each was red-hot. With their eyes on the horizon, they waited. Suddenly they saw Tingararae approaching. Kotisamemba took up position just inside the doorway on the right, and Mimau on the left, their spears held ready. When the giant charged into the house, they drove their spears deep into each side of his neck. With a howl that shook the house from roof to stilts, the monstrous man gave up his life.

Grunting and heaving the brothers dragged Tingararae's massive body to the place of the dead where his spirit would join others and not linger to haunt the house. There they cut him up while Mama Soma started a huge cooking fire. When all was prepared they

invited the men of Arguni to come for a big feast. The guests thought they were eating roast pig, and unwittingly consumed their giant kinsman to the last morsel. Only one man was suspicious and he didn't eat.

During the return voyage to Arguni the men became violently ill. Barely had they reached their village when the last man died, except for the one who did not eat. He threw himself on the sand wailing, *"Ooh!* All our men are dead! *Woh!"* Hearing his lament the women rushed to the shore, pounded the sand in grief and fell wailing upon their men. Amidst the rising dirge, one old woman shouted, "Enough! I will make medicine." From a greasy string pouch she produced some pungent dark leaves. Reciting the names of certain powerful spirits, she touched each man with these magic herbs. The bodies began to stir. Soon everyone was standing and stretching as if they had just awakened from a deep sleep.

The men of Arguni immediately planned to seek revenge against Kotisamemba and Mimau. The two brothers had anticipated retaliation. They had gathered their iron-tipped spears and honed many sturdy bamboo shafts to gleaming sharpness. When Arguni attacked, the spears filled the air like a flock of lorikeets. The brothers fought like a tribe of warriors, although they were only two, and the attackers were driven back to their canoes. The Arguni men returned to their island defeated and demoralized.

The following day they decided to try again. While launching their canoes, a small black and white kwiri-kwiri bird alighted on the lead canoe. "Take me with you, I can give you some advice," said the bird to the leader. He grunted approval and pushed off into the bay. The little bird began to speak, "When we get to the far shore, cut a bough from a senang tree. Strip the branches and peel off the bark to make it very slick. Take down the ladder pole at the house and replace it with the slick bark. When the brothers charge from the house to fight us, they will slip and fall and then we can capture them."

At the first sound of attack, Mimau grabbed his spear and rushed out the door. The ladder pole he stepped on was as slippery as a muddy snake skin. He tumbled like a leaf to the ground, and before his dazed head was clear, he was being carried off, trussed like a pig, toward the enemy's canoe.

Kotisamemba waited one full day, then set out at dusk in his canoe with bow and arrows and a tool for boring holes. The night was dark and moonless as he paddled across the bay. Upon arrival at the beach, he bored holes in each and every canoe. He crept around under the house until he found the room where Mimau was being held. He poked Mimau with a palm frond through the slat floor. Mimau said to his captors, "I have to go out to urinate." He went out, joined his brother and they ran to their canoe. Heading for home they began a loud chant, "*Aoh, Aoh,* Mimau *aka,* Kotisamemba *aka!*" The people scrambled out, sounding the alarm that their captive had escaped. They rushed to their canoes in order to give chase. As they put out to sea, one by one the canoes filled with water and swamped. The men had to give up pursuit and swim back to shore angry and humiliated.

The brothers returned home and celebrated the end of their troubles with the people of Arguni. Mama Soma composed a song summarizing the courage and cleverness of her adopted sons. She sang, "*Ya ware-o rae, Ya ware-o rae.*" (My beloved brave sons.)

From that time on, Kotisamemba and Mimau lived long, fruitful lives as the most esteemed men in all of Bintuni Bay. At the site of ancient Odarewar, near the present village of Goras, where the coast abruptly changes from the calcareous limestone to spongy swamp, there stand two large rock formations known as the Two Brothers. They appeared mysteriously on the very night that Kotisamemba and Mimau died at a ripe old age.

THE ADVENTURES OF FLASSYFLE

Part I

No one knew from where he came, or for how long he had been around. Tales of his exploits and cleverness abounded. He was held in awe by the common people and worshiped as a hero by the children. He was Flassyfle, the first inhabitant of Teminabaum.

His domain was so vast it could not be covered during one full cycle of the moon. The area was dense, lush rain forest covered with trees and vegetation of all kinds. Even in the dry season there was no lack of rain. Spongy green moss softened the jagged limestone hills. Birdsong and tumbling water competed with the constant buzzing of insects that filled the forest with musical sounds. The sunlight, filtering through the leafy canopy, brought out sweet scents of decaying humus and blossoming flowers. Food was plentiful! All life was in balance and harmony!

Flassyfle's house was built high on a hill on a peninsula which meets the sea in steep cliffs. On a clear day he could see a single tree far away on the slopes of the mountains. Many hours were spent in hunting and collecting what he needed for food, but there was always time for exploring, seeking adventures, or just sitting back lost in daydreams. And, of course, there were enemies to be dealt with. Whenever he went anywhere he took a different winding path in order to conceal his tracks and protect himself from ambush.

This clever man knew where game coursed through the jungle. He would often hide along the animal tracks waiting for a wild pig or wallaby or cassowary to come within range of his bow and arrow. Once, when he was so concealed, a thunder squall passed overhead leaving the trees and him drenched with warm rain. Just as he was about to move into a patch of warm sunlight to dry himself, Flassyfle stopped short at the sound of people's voices! Shouting and shrieking could be heard nearby where the ground was moving. He froze and watched anxiously. The earth heaved and cracked open. Out stepped a human being—a man! A great commotion followed. People inside the cleft jostled and pushed trying to get out.

Flassyfle thought quickly; if so many people were allowed to enter his land, surely some of them would be his enemies. All at once, he leaped from his hiding place and confronted the strange man face to face. Startled, the man who had emerged from inside the earth ran to hide in the trees. At that moment the cleft in the ground suddenly closed leaving most of the people trapped. The forest was silent except for the faint cries and moans coming from inside the earth. Soon they disappeared and no sound could be heard.

The underground man presented himself to Flassyfle and humbly asked to be allowed to live in that land. He was called Charin. Flassyfle was moved to the point of accepting him as an adopted son. He regretted his quick-tempered action which had allowed only a few of Charin's clanspeople to escape from inside the earth. The clan of Charin prospered but never grew very large.

Part II

In former times not a single mosquito was to be found in all of Teminabaum. Now, however, the people are plagued night and day by these pesky insects. The responsibility for this great misfortune lies upon Flassyfle himself.

One day Flassyfle set out to wander along the river bank. As usual, he carried his weapons and stone axe slung over his shoulder. He wanted to merely explore and enjoy the natural surroundings. As he was walking along he thought about Charin's relatives and friends who had not escaped from inside the earth. He felt ashamed of his impulsive action which caused them to remain trapped beneath the ground. He wondered what could have possibly happened to them.

Suddenly he was jarred from his thoughts by wrenching and screaming sounds coming from inside a huge mangrove tree. Carefully he bent close to the tree and listened.

"Without a doubt these are human voices," he said. "In fact they must be the lost people of Charin's clan!"

With great excitement he raised his axe to the trunk of the tree. Furiously he swung his axe again and again chopping away at the tree. All he could think of was freeing the lost people and helping them come to the surface of the earth. As he cut closer to the hollow of the tree, he was filled with joy at the thought of greeting them.

Finally Flassyfle reached the inner core of the tree. He was horrified! He had liberated not humans, but hoards of tiny vicious insects. They swarmed around him with a dizzy, deafening sound: zzzzzzzzzzzzz! As if that were not enough, they proceeded to sting and bite him mercilessly.

Flailing his arms about him wildly, he ran away and flung himself into the river. Ever since that day, Teminabaum has been plagued with the annoying creature known now as the nasty mosquito.

Part III

Flassyfle's quick thinking and cleverness saved him many times from falling prey to his enemies. A trick or deception, or last minute escape always saved him from disaster. Many of his people thought he had supernatural powers or was guided by some great spirit.

Once there was a beautiful mango tree with luscious fruit just beginning to ripen. If Flassyfle did not do something soon the birds would certainly come and devour the fruit. He took a gluey type of paste which he decided to spread on the leaves and branches. He climbed high into the mango tree, working diligently unaware that men from an enemy clan had surrounded the tree.

Suddenly he realized the danger he was in. The chief of the enemy clan, with a bone dagger in his hand, was climbing toward him. Unarmed, Flassyfle thought to himself, "I must resign myself to fate. There is no choice." Then like a flash of lightning a plan formed in his mind.

The enemy chief came closer and closer. Flassyfle did not move but looked him straight in the eye and smiled. Casually he continued to apply the sticky glue to the leaves of the tree. Confused by this unexpected reaction the enemy chief halted for a moment. Quick as a darting lizard Flassyfle grabbed the container of glue and dumped it over his enemy's head.

Blinded and startled the man dropped his dagger and tried to wipe the gooey mess from his face. Instantly Flassyfle jumped on him. After a brief struggle, he got a solid strangle hold on the chief and killed him.

The chief's followers watched the tree branches sway and shake furiously, but the leaves were so dense and thick they could not see who was winning the fight. Quickly, Flassyfle changed clothes with the dead chief. He wrapped the corpse in his sarong and covered his face with a scarf. Fortunately Flassyfle was fluent in the enemy's dialect. In a commanding voice he called down to the members of the chief's clan standing beneath the tree.

"Flassyfle is finished! Here, carry his corpse to the boat. Leave all the weapons and equipment. I will bring them when I come. We will meet at the foot of Ayos Hill."

They did as they were told even though the voice sounded somewhat strange and the orders most unusual. But they had been well trained to never question the orders of their chief.

The enemy warriors departed carrying the corpse. All the time they believed it was the dead body of Flassyfle. Their weapons lay scattered underneath the tree.

Flassyfle climbed down from the mango tree, laughing quietly to himself.

"How foolish they are. Look, they even left their weapons," he said. Quickly he gathered up the tools and weapons that he could use and dumped the rest into the river. He must hurry in order to meet them at the designated rendezvous at Ayos Hill.

Seeing their boat in the distance he shouted, "*Hei!* Uncover the head of the corpse and tell me if it is your chief's or mine!"

A shocked moan and howl could be heard at Ayos Hill that day as the warriors looked on the lifeless face of their own chief. Without a leader and afraid of Flassyfle's power they hastily turned the boat in the opposite direction and fled Ayos Hill as fast as possible.

Standing in the cool breeze blowing across the river for a moment, Flassyfle finally turned and started back toward his people's village. The forest echoed with the beating of his small drum and gong. Draped gracefully around his body, he proudly wore the red and blue cloth of victory.

Part IV

Flassyfle often set snares and pit traps in the forest to catch animals. The skins were used for various things and the meat he would use for his food. One day, happy and carefree, he set out to check his traps. He had no premonition that anything threatening might happen to him that day. The sky was clear and the birds were singing cheerily in the trees. All around him spoke only of peace and tranquility.

He crept stealthily to the spot where he had set the traps. Through the trees he saw something that resembled a cassowary bird near one of the traps. How odd that no signs were visible of a cassowary having been snared. No footprints on the ground. No signs of a struggle could be seen anywhere.

Flassyfle looked around carefully. He thought for a moment, then smiled, "Of course. It's not a cassowary. It's a man, an enemy waiting to ambush me."

Glancing around from side to side he spotted others hidden in the bushes. This was undoubtedly revenge for the slaying of their chief near Ayos Hill, he thought.

Quietly, Flassyfle left and walked to the river nearby. He cut many dry pandanus leaves and tied them together with big knots. Each bundle of leaves he then connected with a long vine.

When he had enough he slowly crept back to the place where the traps were set. Without making a sound he placed the string of leaf bunches on the ground around the area where the enemies were hiding.

Suddenly, as if commanding a troop of warriors, Flassyfle leaped forward shouting and gnashing his teeth. Simultaneously he jerked the vine of dry pandanus leaves again and again.

This created a thundering noise that resounded from the hillside and tree-tops. Fearing they were surrounded by hundreds of warriors, the enemy ambushers panicked and scattered in all directions. Some fell into the animal traps, others were mistakenly speared by their own people. Many got caught in thorn bushes or tripped over rocks. The new chief dangled by his neck in the cassowary snare.

Flassyfle had quickly put an end to their surprise attack. It was the last time he had any trouble with that enemy clan.

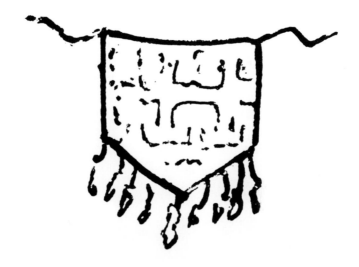

TREE OF RICHES

The old grandmother lived alone in a village with many people. The villagers considered her to be rather odd—an old woman gone full circle back to childhood. She was neglected by all of them except for a few close relatives who supplied her with the barest needs of food and clothing. No one ever came to chat with her. No one ever heard her sing. Each morning she trudged into the forest to search for enough firewood to cook her meager evening meal. The only consolation that made her cheerless life bearable was her precious cockatoo.

The bird was very smart. When he wanted food he would call out, "Yakob is hungry! Yakob is hungry!" After being fed, Yakob would dance and swing on his perch, whistling and squawking. The old woman loved him as she would her own child. If there was not

enough food for both of them, the bird would get his fill while she
held her hunger. For hours at a time she would stroke his golden
crown feathers, whispering sweet words into his ear. She always kept
his water cup full and cleaned his perch whenever he got it messy.

One day the old woman had to go quite far for her firewood.
She filled Yakob's water cup and gave him extra food. The cockatoo
was happy to see so much food. He ate and drank until he was sati-
ated. Then he began to dance. He danced and danced, bobbing and
swinging and jabbering at the top of his voice. His movements were
so excited that all the remaining food spilled to the floor. The same
thing happened to the water. After awhile Yakob stopped to rest. He
was hungry and thirsty but found the cups were empty. He called out,
"Yakob is hungry! Yakob is hungry!" There was no response. The
old woman did not come to pet him and add food to his cup. He called
again and again, but there was no answer. He straightened his dishev-
eled plumage and cleaned his beak. Still no one came. He grew
hungrier and thirstier and his loud squawking grew more and more
desperate. "Yakob is hungry! Yakob is hungry!"

Finally Yakob's rapid breathing slowed to a stop. His eyelids
drooped half-open. His fat pink tongue fell out of the corner of his
beak and he tumbled from his perch, falling lifeless onto the floor of
his cage.

It was late afternoon when the old grandmother returned. She
shuffled slowly from the weariness of her long trek. From outside she
could see that Yakob's leg dangled below his perch by the thong
which bound his leg. "*ADUH! ADUH!*" she cried in anguish,
dropping the load of firewood. She took the lifeless bird in her arms,
rocked back and forth and sobbed. "*Aduh!* My dear Yakob is dead!
My dear Yakob is dead! I might as well die along with him! *Aduh!*"

When her grief finally subsided, the old woman tenderly
wrapped her cockatoo in her best cloth and buried him next to the hut.
From then on her first duty of the day was to tend the tiny grave
making sure it was always kept clean.

One morning, she was surprised to find a small green shoot in the center of the grave. She looked at it carefully and instead of plucking it out, she cleaned all around it and gave it water. Each day the plant grew taller. It had unusually beautiful leaves, unlike any she had ever seen. It grew into a tall, strong tree with lovely spreading branches.

As the other trees in that area began to flower, so too did this exotic tree. Its blossoms were as big as coconuts and filled the air with an hypnotic sweet scent. But the most extraordinary thing happened when the flowers fell and the fruits started to appear. It was quite different from ordinary fruit. The tree became laden with riches! Cloth grew on this tree; shirts, dresses, money, story books, cooking utensils, dishes, tools, flashlights and even a radio and many other things.

There were all the wonderful things that would make life easy and happy for her. The old grandmother danced at her good fortune. For the first time in her miserable life she sang. Her songs were in praise of her dear pet Yakob and she sang about starting a new life as the richest person in the land.

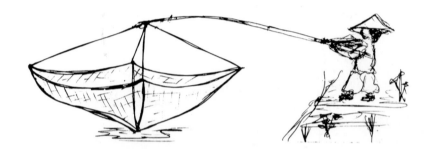

TUU, THE MAGICAL
BAILER SHELL

There was no meat in all the village of Sauwa-Erma. For days the people had been eating sago with the few fish that the women caught each day. One man decided to change this and planned to go hunting. To guarantee success, he brought out his magical bailer shell, Tuu, from its place in the rafters. He fastened the shell to his abdomen, over the right rib cage and set out up-river. Before the sun had dropped below the mangroves, he had returned with a canoe full of meat. He had killed three wild pigs, a cassowary and three large goanna lizards. The villagers praised him for his skill and stood in awe of the power of Tuu.

A few days later the man's younger brother wanted to try his luck with the shell. He told no one of his plans, but secretly took Tuu and tied it around his hip. He felt the shell's power coursing through his body. He paddled in the same direction that his brother had gone some days before. Paddling against the current was tiring and soon he became sleepy. He untied the shell and placed it in the bow, then stretched out in the canoe and fell fast asleep. When he awoke, Tuu was gone!

The younger brother returned to the village dejected and more than a bit worried. He told his brother the bad news, stressing the fact that the shell had run off on its own. Even so, the older brother was extremely angry, and he went off into the jungle to collect a load of firewood. When he returned, the elder brother built a huge bonfire. All the people gathered to see what was going on. All of a sudden the elder brother grabbed his younger brother and flung him into the fire.

The shocked villagers pulled him from the flames and threw him into the river. His entire body was burned. For many days he lay in the house barely alive. His skin peeled and gave off a foul odor. After a long convalescence, he finally recovered.

When he could walk again he went over to see his older brother. He asked about his health and said that as soon as he was strong enough he would order him to go and search for the lost shell. The older brother planned to send his second wife along with his brother to help in the search.

Because the older brother didn't fully trust his younger brother alone with his wife, he devised a test. He placed a discarded canoe hull near the house, filled it with soil, and planted bamboo, banana and sago shoots. He called his brother and second wife and told them, "This will be a sign to me of your activity. If you have any sex along the way, the plants will die, if not, they will live and grow. If you should make love together, Tuu, the shell, will remain lost forever."

During the search in the swamps, the younger brother and the second wife were terribly afraid of having a sexual mishap. They prepared their meals separately and slept far apart.

After four days of combing the tangled roots and myriad waterways of the swamp, they suddenly spotted the shell on the surface of the water. Overcome with excitement, the young man jumped into the stream to capture it. Tuu, however, was quicker and disappeared under water.

The younger brother was afraid to return without the shell. They stayed several more days. Tuu would appear and as soon as the younger brother would dive for it, the shell disappeared. One day Tuu was seen resting on a branch over the river's edge. The man told his sister-in-law to creep up on the shell with her net. He hurried downstream with another net. When the shell dove into the water, they were able to trap it in their nets. Tuu thrashed about like a stingray, but they held on and finally subdued it.

They paddled back to the village, Tuu secure in the canoe. The first thing they did was to check the little garden in the canoe hull. It was filled with healthy plants. The elder brother was overjoyed that the shell had been returned and that his wife had not been molested. He praised his brother on both counts and promised a great feast for the whole village on the following day.

What a feast it was! They had pig meat, fresh fish, sago cakes, and fruit from the plants in the canoe hull. Men and women ate together for the first time. They all agreed it was no longer necessary for them to eat separately, or forbid women to eat in the longhouse.

The occasion was one of real joy and celebration. The elder brother said that from now on the younger brother should take his second wife as his own. At first, the younger brother refused this generous offer, but quickly accepted when the elder brother said he would kill him if he didn't!

From then on there was always harmony between the two brothers. They were constant companions when fishing and hunting and were always aided by the magical shell, Tuu. They became the greatest hunters on the Pomatsj River.

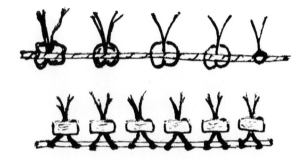

TANT RIDAH

Long ago, in the village of Tabati, lived a man, his wife and their son whose name was Tant Ridah. He was thirteen years old, still a boy but soon to become a man. He had many friends his age and they would often go places and do things together.

One day these friends planned a trek to the mouth of the river. They brought all the food and supplies necessary for a day's outing and set off full of enthusiasm! When they arrived at the mouth of the river, they stripped off their clothes and jumped into the cool water. They swam and played until the sun was past the middle of the sky. They were all really hungry. Sitting under a tree by the water, they opened their food bundles and passed around the baked sago, fish and fruit.

   Just as Tant Ridah was about to enjoy his food, he discovered
that the necklace he had been wearing was no longer around his neck.
This worried him because his mother had given it to him when he was
a small boy. He had been told to look after the necklace very carefully

because it was an heirloom from his grandmother. He thought and thought about where he might have lost it. Finally he decided that it must have broken while he was swimming and sunk to the bottom of the river. Tant Ridah began to dive for the missing necklace. After diving again and again he had found only about one-half of the beads and could find no more. He took the beads, strung them on a bit of vine and returned home feeling sad and guilty.

Having reached the house, Tant Ridah would now have to face his mother. "Mama, the necklace from my grandmother is not complete anymore." His mother became very angry when she saw that only half the beads were there. As her anger increased she began cursing him. Finally she grabbed a piece of seroang wood resembling a sword with two eyes and threatened to give him a good thrashing. His father heard the commotion. When he learned what had happened he joined his wife in her anger and went after Tant Ridah with a long cassowary bone. The frightened boy managed to escape and fled to his grandmother's house.

"I beg your forgiveness grandmother," he pleaded, "I have done a terribly wrong thing." He told her what had happened regarding the necklace. His grandmother listened patiently, and was filled with loving pity for her grandson. When he had finished she told him what he must do.

"You must prepare to leave here and go live on the island of Sori," she said. Across the straits from Tant Ridah's village was a mysterious island. Peculiar things happened to people who visited there. The most unusual thing was that it was inhabited solely by women. They were the descendants of Sori, who in the past had used her powerful magic to cause all the men to disappear. Sori's closest living relative was the lovely maiden, Feschoi Faschoi. The women became pregnant by occasionally meeting mainland men as they went out hunting and fishing. At the time of birth the mother was assisted by other women who cut open her stomach with a knife and removed the baby. If the baby was a boy it was immediately killed. This was their custom, even to that day.

Just before Tant Ridah set out in his canoe for that strange island his grandmother gave him this advice. "When you arrive, pay careful attention to the banyan trees that grow along the shore. Do not approach the places where the trees are not thick and leafy. The spirit inhabitants of such trees like to eat people. If you see trees with abundant foliage you may land because those spirits are of good heart. They like to help people."

The sun was high overhead when Tant Ridah pointed his outrigger in the direction of Sori. With a fair wind filling the plaited frond sail, he arrived offshore just before dusk. He paddled along the shore looking for a suitable place to land. Where the banyan tree leaves were sparse he turned his canoe back toward the sea, ignoring the trees inviting calls. He knew from his grandmother's warning that those trees were waiting to capture and devour him.

Finally he sighted a banyan tree with thick, leafy foliage. He landed and was welcomed by the spirit inhabitants of that tree. Clearly they were good spirits. Concerned about his welfare, they advised Tant Ridah to hide in a nearby bitanggur tree. They shared food with him and told him many things about the island. Tant Ridah learned that every morning after sunrise all the important women of the village came to that beach to bathe.

When dawn broke the next day, Tant Ridah saw a beautiful girl coming to the beach. Without a doubt this must be Feschoi Faschoi. He picked a bitanggur fruit and tossed it at the girl. Eyes wide with surprise and fear, she looked right and left to see where the fruit had come from. Tant Ridah tossed another one. This time Feschoi Faschoi spotted him up in the tree and was astonished. "Who are you? Where have you come from?" she demanded.

"My name is Tant Ridah, child of Tant Diens and Monj Jackol. I have come to your island upon the instruction of my grand-mother." After the introductions, the young woman escorted Tant Ridah to her house without the knowledge of the other women. After three or four months of living secretly with Feschoi Faschoi he realized that she was pregnant. When it was time for her to give birth

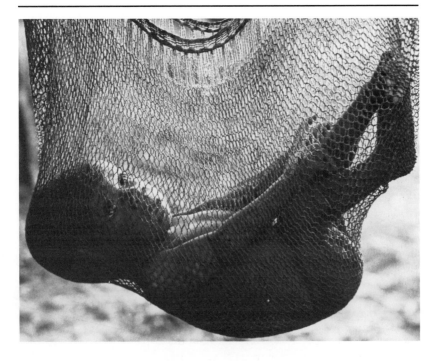

several women gathered in the house to assist her. They were astonished to find a strong handsome man living with her. For a moment it
was very quiet and no one had a word to say.

Then Tant Ridah stepped forward and introduced himself. He
told them the whole story and explained how it came about that he
was on their island. Afterwards, he instructed the women in the proper
ways of helping in the birth of a baby and the care for an infant. He
told them how wrong it was to kill male babies and explained how
their lives might benefit from the presence of men on their island.

Following the guidance of Tant Ridah and with the assistance
of the women, a baby boy was safely born on the island of Sori
without injury to either the mother or child. From that day on the
population of that island grew and the people prospered. The killing
of boy babies stopped at that time and was never again practiced on
that island.

THE MOON'S REVENGE

Inay and his wife lived some distance from the village. They chose to live here so they could be near their garden. Inay and his wife had worked hard day after day preparing the soil and caring for the plants. The land, in turn, yielded the finest yams, beans, bananas, papayas, sugar-cane. Everything was good to eat. A pond, which provided water for Inay's garden, bordered their plot.

Early one morning, about the time of the full moon, Inay came to the garden and found that it had been ravished. The ripe fruits and vegetables ready to be harvested had been stolen. No signs or tracks of an intruder could be seen anywhere.

Inay suspected someone of the village was responsible for the theft. But after questioning everyone in each household and finding no guilt on anyone's face, he was mystified. He decided to go to his trusted friend Irouma and ask for help. That evening Inay wrapped Irouma in leaves and hid him in the hollow of a tree near the garden entrance. Inay returned home while his friend stayed to begin his night watch for the return of the thief.

Soon after sunset, when shadows faded and night crept over the forest, the moon appeared on the face of the pond. Slowly it drifted across the water and entered the garden gate. Irouma watched astonished as the moon collected the remaining ripe fruits and vegetables. Then the moon disappeared into the darkness. Irouma was still trembling with fear when Inay arrived at dawn to hear him tell of the night's experience.

"*Ah*, so it was the moon! How very strange," said Inay. He decided that the only way to save his garden was to capture the moon.

Inay sent word to all the women of the village, "Go to the sago groves and collect enough flour for all of us. Then come to my house for a feast of pepeda and fresh vegetables." During the meal he told them how the moon hid in his pond and then stole his fresh produce at night. He told them of a plan to catch the moon using large fish nets. The women all agreed to help. In fact, each one was secretly eager to capture it and keep it for herself.

Now just before they set out for the pond, Inay whispered to his wife and told her the exact spot where the moon first appeared in the water. With great care they all placed themselves strategically around the pond. The crucial moment came and the women dipped their nets where each thought they saw the moon. All they had were reflections of the moon. Inay's wife was just where her husband had indicated and with her first swoop of the net, caught the moon. Quickly she hid the glowing sphere in the grass. She didn't want the other women to know about it. After a short time she said, "I am cold, I will go in and get warm." Concealing the moon beneath her sarong, she returned to the house. Carefully she placed it in a large earthen jar

and covered it with an old Chinese plate. Many nights after the event, Inay and his wife enjoyed the bright rays of the moon which filled their house with a golden glow whenever they removed the cover of the jar.

One day Inay's grandson and his friends came to visit. The children played in the house while Inay and his wife went to the garden. Before long the children discovered the moon in the earthen jar. "What a perfect target for our little bows and arrows," they said. They lifted the plate off the jar. As the moon rose from the jar they shot arrows at it. It slipped out the door and continued to drift upward to the top of a coconut tree. From that height the moon's brightness shone over the entire valley.

Inay and his wife saw the light and were alarmed. "The moon must have escaped," they gasped. He rushed back to the house. Indeed it was gone from the earthen jar. There it was high above the coconut tree. Furious, Inay called out a curse to the moon, "When you reach your place in the sky, you shall remain below the sun!" The moon replied, "Listen carefully to my words. Whenever I rise red in the east and glow red in the night sky, the hand of death will strike your family, or your unborn child will die. This not all. Because your grandson and friends pierced me with arrows, every month I will send the moon sickness on all of your women."

Not only did these harsh words come to pass, but the trouble with the moon caused the separation of Inay and his wife.

HOW STARS
BECAME FIREFLIES

In ancient times, when the spirits of today were our living ancestors, there lived a man named Kokwab. He had an unusual appetite. Every night after sunset he left the village with a bag of freshly cooked sago balls. He would go to the forest where he visited a particular coconut tree. When he reached the tree he spoke kindly, "Coconut tree, my friend, you are so beautiful. You know I like you very much. Please bend over so I can sit in your top branches."

The tree obeyed and bent over until its top fronds touched the ground. Kokwab climbed on and sat down. When the tree stood upright again Kokwab rubbed its trunk with a special leaf. As he rubbed, the tree grew taller and taller. He continued rubbing until the

top branches touched the sky. Then he stepped off and told the tree, "Now you can return to your normal height, but before dawn you must grow tall again so I can return to earth."

High up in the sky Kokwab happily wandered about plucking stars and mixing them with his sago balls. All night long he feasted on the star-studded sago, almost to the bursting point.

Just before dawn he called to the coconut tree begging it to grow tall so he could descend back to earth. The tree did as it was told and Kokwab came down and returned to his village. He was very sleepy because he had eaten so much. Straight to his house he went and there he slept all day long.

Night after night, Kokwab rode the coconut tree to the sky and feasted on stars and sago. He took great care to set out after sunset and return before sunrise. This way no one knew he had left the village.

After a time the coconut tree grew bored and irritated, ferrying Kokwab to and from the sky every night. Besides, Kokwab never gave the tree any reward for his efforts and hard work. So one night, after Kokwab had eaten his fill of sago and stars, the tree refused to grow tall again. Kokwab pleaded and threatened, all to no avail.

Finally, he had no choice but to leap from the sky to the earth. He landed with a mighty splash in the middle of a river. The force of his fall was so great that his abdomen split open. All the stars he had eaten were scattered among the mangrove trees that lined the river banks.

It is fortunate for us that Kokwab met this fate. If not, who knows, there would not be any stars left in the heavens. Only very few stars are left in the area just above the horizon. The stars that were there long ago have been eaten by Kokwab. Those stars were released by Kokwab's great fall from the sky and remain sparkling in the mangroves to this day. Now we call them "*bak* " (fireflies).

ORIGIN OF
THE COCONUT TREE

Once upon a time a group of children played along the muddy river bank of Warse. They caught small mud fish and wrapped them in leaves. They had been playing for a few hours when Tsjuperei joined them.

"What do you have wrapped in the leaves?" he asked.

"Each one of us has a clitoris wrapped in this little bundle," they answered.

Tsjuperei ran home and begged his mother for her clitoris so that he could join the other children in their game. He cried and cried

and finally his mother gave in. She took a small shell knife and cut it off and gave it to her son.

That night, while lying with his wife, Tsjuperei's father discovered a lot of blood on the sleeping mat. He shouted, "Where is all this blood from? Do you have the moon sickness?"

"It is nothing," she answered, "I gave my clitoris to our son so he could play with the other children down by the river."

Tsjuperei's father was outraged. The next morning his anger had still not subsided. He went down to the swamps and searched among the aerial roots until he found a large python. He brought it back and hid it in the corner of the house.

"What do you want with me?" asked the snake. "Only this," said the father. "Listen carefully. Here is where my son sleeps. During the night you must bite him on the nose, coil yourself around his body until he has no more breath."

"But I don't want to harm this young boy," said the snake.

"Do as I say or I will cut off your head," cried the father.

In the morning there was weeping and wailing in the village. The snake was gone and poor Tsjuperei was lying lifeless on his sleeping mat.

The brothers-in-law of the family took his body and buried him in front of the men's long-house. The body was placed in such a manner that the head was left sticking up out of the ground. All day long the drums of mourning sounded their slow, steady beat. In the afternoon the sky grew dark and ominous. Thick black clouds rolled over the tops of the mangrove trees. Throughout the night thunder and lightning crashed and the rain poured down in torrents.

During the tempest and heavy storm Tsjuperei's head began to sprout. In the morning the members of the Warse clan were astonished to find a tall tree standing exactly on the spot where Tsjuperei was buried. The tree was loaded with strange and unfamiliar fruit.

The people hurried to gather a lot of sago and catch some fish for a big feast. All the next day there was drumming and dancing in celebration of the miraculous event that had taken place.

They gathered some of the fruit from the tree and prepared it. The in-laws of Tsjuperei were given the privilege of tasting the fruit first.

"It's delicious," they exclaimed. "It's soft and sweet and slides smoothly down the throat." One after another, all the members of the Warse clan ate from the first coconut tree.

To this day, in a wide area surrounding Warse, when people eat a coconut they say they are eating the head of Tsjuperei.

EBI AND KANDEI

Ebi is a bird, a scissortail, and Kandei is a fresh water fish, no longer than ten centimeters.

One day Ebi went to the edge of the lake and dug up a piece of land for a garden. He planted a variety of bananas and vegetables that could be eaten by human beings as well as by animals. A type of banana that he planted was one which would yield fruit in about three to four months. That tree was called *"pisang tanduk"* or horned banana. Every day he pulled the grass and weeds that grew around this tree. When it was three months old the fruit started looking yellow.

About that time, Kandei came to the place where the banana tree stood. He looked at it and longed to eat the fruit. So he cut down the tree and carried it to his home. When he got to his house, he prepared the wood, built a fire and then baked the bananas. The smoke rose up in the air, and Ebi, the owner of the banana tree could see where the smoke was coming from. The clouds of smoke were visible from a great distance. Ebi checked his garden and saw that the tree had been cut and stolen. He followed the tracks of the thief. It brought him to the house of Kandei and as luck would have it, there he sat eating the baked bananas. Kandei was frightened and angry when he saw Ebi coming to his house. Ebi walked in and saw the bananas. What should he do? The bananas were his.

Being very hungry, he asked if he could have one. Kandei gave him one and he peeled it. Kandei wiped his eyes because of the smoke from the fire. Suddenly Ebi exclaimed in a startled manner, "Oh my goodness, there is a lump of dirt or an insect on your eyelid, my friend Kandei!"

Hearing the words of Ebi, Kandei became alarmed. He rubbed and rubbed his eyes trying to get the dirt off. Then Ebi took the hot banana which he had just peeled and pressed it very hard into Kandei's eye. Kandei screamed, squirming and turning every which way because of the pain. He ran and jumped into the lake searching for a peaceful quiet place for protection. Fortunately, a large fish lived in the waters nearby. His name was Hinem and he was very old.

Kandei entered under the chin of Hinem and slept there hoping to regain his health and be completely healed. Hinem read several incantations and breathed on Kandei's wound. In just a few days the pain began to subside. Gradually he regained his strength and was well again. After thanking Hinem, Kandei swam back to his home near the lake.

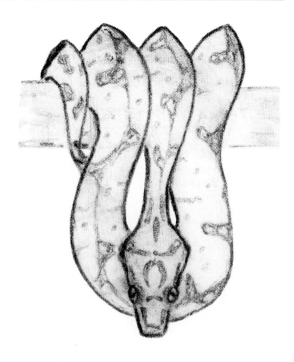

HOW PEOPLE
CAME TO EAT PIG

Long ago in the village of Sauwa, there lived a snake. It was a rather short but thick and powerful snake. His name has been long forgotten, but he will always be remembered for his cleverness. For years and years this snake had looked after a particular perahu tree, waiting for the day when it would be big enough to be carved into a fine canoe.

Finally the long awaited day arrived. The tree was tall and shaped perfectly. The snake cut it down, hollowed out the log and shaped it well. Then he burnt it with fire to lighten it. The last touches of decorating it with carved relief and earthen paint were done with the greatest care. How beautiful it was and how proud he felt when he saw the finished canoe.

He launched it with due ceremony and paddled out into the river. How pleased he was with his well-made craft.

It so happened that a certain spirit also had his eye on the perahu tree which the snake had cut down. When he saw the snake at work cutting down the tree the spirit thought, "Better to let the snake do all the work. When he is finished I will take my revenge on him and steal the canoe."

So when the snake, tired from paddling his beautiful new canoe, came ashore, the spirit was there to meet him.

"Hi, snake, you look beautiful to me. Come let us make passionate love together." The spirit's greeting seemed friendly enough, but somehow the snake was suspicious. Besides that, he wasn't the least bit interested in the proposal. However, one must be careful when dealing with a spirit. So he replied, "*Ayo,* spirit, let's go! You gather some soft leaves for us to lie on."

While the spirit was busy spreading leaves on the muddy ground, the snake made a dash for the canoe and pushed off into

midstream. He called to the angry, fuming spirit on the shore, "Why do you want to have intercourse with me anyway? I am a snake, not a woman."

The spirit yelled back at him, "You will not get away with this trick. Tonight I will come to your house!"

When the snake got home he blocked up every hole in the house except the main entrance. He piled a lot of dried leaves there. Then he strung his strongest bow and sharpened his arrows. In the evening the snake and his family ate their meal. Then everyone went to sleep except the snake.

After it was very dark, the spirit approached the entrance of the snake's house. Carefully he pushed aside some of the leaves and waited. Nothing happened. The spirit pushed aside more leaves. Still nothing happened. The remaining leaves were pushed aside and he stepped through the doorway. At that instant the snake fired his arrow from a dark corner. The arrow pierced the spirit's right armpit and stuck out from his left armpit. The spirit howled in agony and fled into the forest. As he ran down the path the snake called after him, "You will become a pig, you will become a pig!"

Early the next morning the snake followed the trail of blood. Soon he came upon a pig with his own arrow through its chest. He called his family and relatives and together they cut up the pig. First the front legs were cut off, then the hind legs, finally the body was divided.

When all the cutting of the pig was completed, they built a huge fire to roast a piece of the meat. The snake gave this piece to his son-in-law. After eating it, the unfortunate son-in-law immediately dropped dead on the spot where the pig had been butchered.

The snake then told all his family to follow him into his house. There the meat was cooked and everyone ate of it. No one died. Then the snake declared in a solemn tone of voice, "All Asmat people may eat pig." And from that day on, all Asmats have eaten pig during their ceremonies and festivals. And all spirits became pigs.

THE BEWITCHED
CASUARINA TREE

In the central highlands of Irian Jaya, people live in fenced clusters of beehive-shaped houses. They lie scattered throughout the valley and rise up into the foothills of the towering mountains. In one such hamlet, set around a majestic casuarina tree, the clan was puzzled by a recurring mysterious happening. At sundown the women returned from their gardens. Their net bags were full of yams, ferns and sugar cane. They prepared food for the evening meal and enough for their next morning's meal. However at sunrise they would find that most of the food had disappeared. Sometimes even a pig was missing. "Who could be taking all of this food?" they wondered.

First they suspected a neighboring clan might be responsible for the thefts. On second thought this seemed highly unlikely. How was it possible for someone to creep into the compound and take the food from the doorways without waking anyone? Furthermore, each hamlet had its own productive gardens. There was no need to steal food. The clan decided the culprits must be ghosts.

A night watch was organized to see if this was true. The first two nights the watchmen fell asleep at their post inside the pig shed. The food vanished as usual. But the guard standing watch the third night witnessed an extraordinary event! From inside the branches of the huge casuarina tree which stood in the center of the compound, emerged a group of men. They materialized one after another right in front of his eyes. Each one was young and handsome. Their strong warrior bodies glistened with pig fat. Rings of bright white cockatoo feathers adorned their heads and wide bibs of tiny nassa shells hanging on their chests glowed in the pale moonlight. Their *koteka* (penis sheaths) were long ceremonial ones tipped with a squirrel's tail or a piece of cuscus fur. They carried no weapons.

Although they appeared to be walking and talking together, they made no sound. They went straight to the net bags filled with yams and greens, helping themselves to as much as they wanted. Gathering around the trunk of the great tree, they ate their fill. Sitting back satisfied, they sucked on freshly rolled tobacco leaves.

As the moon sank beneath the horizon, they quietly returned to their tree home, fusing completely with the bark of the branches.

At the crack of dawn, the astounded watchman aroused all the members of the clan and related the incredible sight he had witnessed. They discussed the situation and then all agreed, "Yes, we must chop down the bewitched tree at once!"

So it came to pass that the casuarina tree was felled. Its branches were thrown into the river with hopes that the ghost inhabitants would drown in the swift current.

But that was not to be the end of those splendid young spirit men. The branches of the great casuarina tree floated far downstream. They finally came to rest on the river bank in a valley called

Bokondini. The driftwood had lain there just two days when a group of women came by collecting firewood. They gathered the branches of the mysterious tree. When they returned to the compound, they placed them outside the houses in order to dry.

At dawn the women noticed the strange disappearance of their morning food. They discussed the situation and decided on the very same plan used by the neighboring tribe up the river, with slight variations. Women would stand guard and there would be one person watching in each hut.

As had been agreed, a woman in each hut stayed awake and kept secret watch on her food supply. That night, the young men of the tree branches materialized once again as before. But when the men tried to sneak into the hut to steal the food, the women embraced them one by one. They saw how strong and handsome they were and claimed them as their husbands. Great feasting followed for days.

The empty casuarina branches were used as fuel in the pit ovens of the collective marriage feast. The families grew and prospered and lived happily ever after. To this day the descendants of those marriages are the present residents of Bokondini Valley.

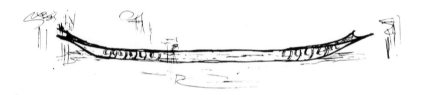

THE SQUIRREL
AND THE TERRAPIN

The following is a tale told by the people of Sentani.
Long ago there lived a squirrel and a terrapin who were great friends.
They were such close friends that wherever they went, they went
together; whatever they did, they did together.

One day these two decided to go across the lake in search of
some delicious shellfish. Down to the lakeside they scrambled and got
into their small dugout canoe. They were excited and full of enthusiasm as they paddled away towards a point of land called Buyebi Dei
Yebi.

During their journey, Terrapin spotted a coconut bobbing up
and down in the lake. Quickly they steered the canoe alongside the

coconut. Squirrel reached for it and brought it on board. The companions were overjoyed at their good fortune. This was not only refreshment for later, but also a favorable omen. Right then and there, they made a promise, "After collecting plenty of shellfish we will divide the coconut and enjoy it together."

Upon arrival at the place called Buyebi Dei Yebi they entered a small cove where someone had put up a fence to catch fish. The canoe was fastened to one of these stakes. Quickly, they took off their clothes and jumped into the water. Moments later they came to the surface with lots of shellfish. All morning they dove for the mollusks and piled them into the canoe until it was full.

They had been in the water quite a long time. Squirrel began to feel cold and started to shiver. He called to Terrapin and said, "I'm going to the canoe to warm up and rest a bit." While he was basking in the sun he began to feel hungry. Squirrel took the coconut and looked at it longingly. Then, not caring about the promise made earlier with his friend, he bored a hole in the coconut with his sharp teeth. Greedily, he gobbled up all the fresh juice and the tasty white meat of the fruit.

Even though turtle was under water, he could hear the noise of Squirrel's sharp teeth gnawing the hard coconut shell. He rose to the surface of the lake and asked, "What noise deafened my ears underwater?"

Somewhat startled, but thinking quickly, Squirrel answered, "Truly it was nothing I did. But according to the ancient stories about this place called Buyebi Dei Yebi, if anyone hears strange sounds while underwater, they will become sacred."

Terrapin was getting cold so he climbed into the canoe. While warming himself, he also felt hungry and reached for the coconut. How surprised he was to find a hole in the husk and nothing inside.

"Who did this?" he shouted. Squirrel remained silent. This shameful behavior only made Terrapin more angry. He knew who the guilty one was. Finally in a feeble but pleading tone of voice, Squirrel

begged, "Come, let's go to the coconut plantation. There I will gather as many coconuts for you as you want." Terrapin's anger subsided and they rode off in the direction of the plantation.

When they reached the plantation Squirrel jumped on shore while Terrapin waited in the canoe. Squirrel climbed up a tall coconut tree loaded with fruit. A moment later coconuts began thumping to the ground. Some rolled into the water where Terrapin could easily catch them. People passing by picked up those that fell on the grass.

Soon Heki Boki, the owner of the plantation became aware of what Squirrel was up to. He ordered him to come down from the tree immediately! The order was not heeded. Heki Boki cursed the squirrels of the world and vowed that he would kill every last one of them.

Overcome with rage, Heki Boki took his axe and began chopping the tree down. He figured that by felling the coconut tree he would be able to kill the squirrel. Clearly his efforts were in vain. As soon as Squirrel felt the tree beginning to topple, he jumped over to the next tree. As soon as that tree was about to fall he jumped to yet another, and on and on until every last tree in the coconut plantation was destroyed. As the last one was falling he leapt to a branch of a huge ironwood tree. There he sat, laughing at the foolish Heki Boki.

Weary and full of remorse, the sad plantation owner returned to his house to ponder his unfortunate fate.

What about Squirrel's friend Terrapin? Well, he stuffed himself with fresh coconut and swam back to the bottom of the lake, enjoying his own peace and quiet.

THE SPIRIT
AND THE SONS OF JILIK

Long ago there lived a man named Jilik. He and a spirit used the same area to collect sago. They cut the trees at different times and therefore had never met one another.

One day Jilik cut down a particularly large and fertile sago palm tree. Assisted by his five wives and five sons, he began to peel open the trunk to get at the starchy pith inside. It would take them several days to get all the starch from that big tree.

This particular palm tree happened to be one the spirit had long considered his. He was furious that Jilik had harvested it. "I must go after him and get him for this," whispered the spirit to himself. He set out after him. The enraged spirit approaching through the swamp sounded like a terrible thunderstorm beating down on the canopy of the jungle.

Jilik was terrified. He called to his five wives and told them to take their infants and hide in a grove of Nipa palms. His five grown sons were also given orders to hide.

Total revenge beat in the heart of the spirit. Upon arrival at Jilik's place, he cut down some old trees and made a huge fire. Before long he found the five wives with their babies. He cooked them on the fire and ate them.

After witnessing all this, Jilik told his five sons to run for their lives. Then, in a frenzy, he raised his axe and dealt the spirit a crushing blow to the back of his head. It was a blow that would have debrained a crocodile. However, the spirit merely shrugged it off and turned on Jilik. In no time at all, Jilik was also cooked and eaten. Then the spirit set out in pursuit of the five sons.

The spirit followed the tracks of the five young men until sunset. Here he was stopped by a river. Too tired to swim across, he made a simple bivouac and spent the night there. He didn't know the sons of Jilik were in a bivouac just across the river.

The five sons had only one ball of sago between them, but it proved to be enough. When the sago ball was roasted on the outside, the eldest peeled off a layer as his portion. Then he returned it to the fire until the outside layer was roasted. The second son took this portion. The sago ball was again returned to the fire and roasted and the third son ate. This went on until all were satisfied. They wrapped the remaining lump of sago in some special leaves. In a wondrous manner the lump of sago was restored to its original size, ready to feed them the following day.

The spirit woke about mid-day. He crossed the river and found the brothers' bivouac. A sound like human voices came from inside. With a bloodthirsty cry, he burst into the hut. It was empty. All

he had disturbed was a swarm of flies whose buzzing he had mistaken for human voices. The five sons, sensing that the spirit was not far behind, had left early that morning.

As his anger increased, the spirit continued his search for the men. He traveled a full day and at sunset reached another river. Once again, the spirit was too lazy to cross the river; he spent the night on the shore. Just across the river the five sons were bivouacked for the night. As before, the brothers set out early the next morning while the spirit crossed the river at mid-day. Fooled a second time by the buzzing of flies, he burst in on an empty bivouac. This pattern continued for many days. Each time his anger increased and it began to unhinge the spirit.

One afternoon the sons of Jilik came to a very wide and swift-flowing river. It was impossible to swim across! A large turtle basked in the water nearby. As soon as the turtle saw the men it dove beneath the surface of the water. They called to it gently and persuasively and eventually the turtle emerged.

"Are there any *tisir* spirits living in the river?" they asked the turtle. They knew full well that if they did not respect the *tisir* it would swallow them. The turtle replied, "Yes, indeed, a *tisir* spirit does live in these waters."

"Would you be so kind and ask the *tisir* spirit to help us across the river?" pleaded the young men. They explained their predicament in detail. The turtle listened carefully, then disappeared to the bottom of the river.

Soon the turtle returned with this message: "The *tisir* agrees to help you, but do not be afraid when she surfaces!"

Suddenly there was a great burst of water, waves splashed against the muddy bank and a gigantic fish-like creature appeared! The young men gasped in awe. Never before had they been so close to a *tisir*. Politely they explained how their mothers and father had been eaten by a spirit. "May we consider you, *tisir*, and you, turtle, as our new mother and father?" they begged. *Tisir* and turtle agreed to

become their new parents. The men were told to ride on *tisir's* back
and were taken safely across to the other shore. *Tisir* also agreed to
remain with them and help deal with the spirit when he would come
in search of them.

As expected, a short time later, the spirit arrived at the river.
"*Tisir*, come here and carry me across the river," he demanded. The
five sons stood on the opposite shore and watched tisir go and fetch
the spirit. When they reached the middle of the river *Tisir* turned over
and forced the spirit underwater. A tremendous fight followed. The
waters churned and foamed. Waves splashed against the bank greatly
widening the river. A wild turbulent whirlpool surged around the
place where tisir finally dragged the spirit under and drowned him.

The sons of Jilik thanked their new father, *tisir*, and bade
farewell to their new mother, the turtle, and went their way. At dusk
while the others built a bivouac for the night, the eldest wandered off
with bow and arrow to hunt for game. Nearby he came upon five
women pounding sago.

"What are your names?" he asked. At first they did not
answer. When they realized he meant them no harm they told him that
they were the wives of Wobunuh. Jilik's oldest son explained how he
and his four brothers came to be in this area. The women listened with
great sympathy. The story excited them. They said, "Come back
tomorrow with your bow and arrow. We want you to kill Wobunuh,
our husband." Before he left, the women presented him with five
balls of sago. He quickly returned to his brothers and told them what
had happened. Then he gave to each one his surprise gift of sago.

The next day, as had been agreed, the eldest son returned to
meet the women. Secretly they showed him how to best ambush
Wobunuh. He was out hunting wild game. The son of Jilik carefully
followed the instructions of the women and with one arrow to the
heart, he killed Wobunuh. The body fell into the river; the deed was
done.

The five women came and started fishing with their nets.
They caught shrimp and other fish. Wobunuh, who had turned into a

pig, was also dragged up from the bottom of the river. All feasted on the shrimp and fish, but only the men ate the flesh of the pig.

The five sons of Jilik and the five wives of Wobunuh remained together as husbands and wives and lived happily ever after. This marked the beginning of a new settlement and the continuation of Jilik's clan.

ORIGIN OF
THE JAGIRO CLAN

Originally only four people lived on the east side of the Sebiyar River. The area was called Lawara. There was Nenek, the grandmother; Kakak, the elder brother; Adik, the younger brother; and Ipar, the elder brother's wife. They lived high in a tree house protected from their enemies across the river.

One day while Ipar was preparing a goanna lizard for the evening meal, Adik caught a long look at her privates, under her tapa skirt. He picked up a lump of charcoal from the firepit and climbed down to the outhouse. There, on the bark walls, he began to draw what he had seen. He became so absorbed in his drawing that when his brother called him to eat, he didn't come. He shouted, "Go ahead, you eat first. I'll come later." Finally after satisfying his artistic urge, Adik came to eat.

Kakak, curious as to what had involved his younger brother so long in the outhouse, went down to investigate. When he saw the drawings he thought, "*Awoi!* Adik has been spying on my wife. It must have been a long time to know such detail." He wanted to beat his brother then and there, but his anger cooled as another plan formed in his mind.

The following day Kakak called Adik. "Come join me. We will go across the river to raid an enemy house in Ayamaru." The raid was successful. The inhabitants fled. Kakak and Adik plundered their weapons, tools and utensils and left.

When they reached the river Kakak ordered Adik, "You remain on guard while I take the spoils across the river. I will return with the raft to fetch you." However, when Kakak reached the other side he unloaded the raft and kicked it back into the current and returned home alone. Adik was stranded on the enemy side of the Lawara.

"Where is Adik?" asked Nenek.

"Oh, he's coming. He was going too slow for me," Kakak answered.

Nenek waited and waited but still no Adik. Finally she went out and followed the trail to the river. She shouted, "Adik, where are you?" He answered clear and loud. Nenek quickly cut a rattan vine and ordered it to cross the river. Adik climbed aboard, but the leaf immediately sank. Then Nenek ordered a dry chunk of batan wood across, but this also sank when Adik tried to board it. The third try worked when she sent a log from a mesroho tree. Adik climbed on it and was carried safely to the other shore.

Nenek joined him on the big log and they went downstream on the Lawara River. They had traveled a long time before Nenek chose a place to stop. They went ashore. Nenek instructed Adik, "Cut down a tall tree and build a longhouse."

After felling the tree he began construction immediately. He worked for days and days building the great longhouse. It was divided

into many rooms according to his grandmother's instructions. Finally he came and told his grandmother that he had finished the task she had ordered him to do.

"Good!" she replied. "Now you must kill me."

Adik was dumbfounded. "I cannot kill you! You are my grandmother. I care for you too much!" She replied firmly, "Never mind. You must do as I tell you! But now, listen carefully and do exactly as I tell you. After you kill me cut up all my flesh. Place a piece of it, wrapped in tobacco leaves, in each room of the longhouse. Throw my liver, gall bladder, and intestines in the river. Keep my heart and nose with you in the middle room. Now kill me."

A long silence followed, then with fear and great sadness Adik did all he had been commanded by his grandmother.

By nightfall he was astonished to find each room filled with people. They were happily smoking tobacco. He was bewildered. "How can this be?" he thought. A further surprise awaited him when he looked to his right and to his left, where he had placed the heart and nose. There, on his right and on his left, stood two lovely maidens. They smiled at him and said, "We are your wives."

Adik didn't talk to anyone. He didn't even close the door to his room. All night he sat there stupefied. At sunrise the people left, in small groups heading into the jungle in all directions. Soon the longhouse was empty. Only Adik and his wives remained.

The people that had appeared mysteriously in the longhouse that evening spread far and wide. They became the tribes of Irian that are known today. Grandmother's viscera drifted across the seas to become the white people of the world. Adik and his wives founded a great clan which can still be found today living in the place called Jagiro.

SUSPICIOUS OLD WOMAN

Many years ago an old woman lived on the island of Biak. One of her greatest joys in life was chewing betel nut. If she couldn't chew betel she wouldn't eat. In other words betel nut was more important to her than food.

She made her living by tilling the soil and gathering sago. The crops were not very good but apparently sufficient to provide for her daily needs, at least most of them.

The old woman lived near the beach. When it was low tide she and the other women from the village would go look for fish and shells along the shore. Many large, medium size and small fish would be caught. Then the women carried them home, happy and content with their catch. Later the fish were cleaned, barbecued or cooked in a broth and enjoyed by all the family members in the village.

One morning before sunrise the old woman got up and prepared all she needed for catching fish. She had eaten breakfast quickly because it was low tide. This was the best time to find many fish in among the seashells. All the women of the village hurried to the beach hoping to get a big catch. There were many boats in the sea near the shore; men as well as women were out there that morning, busy hauling in as many fish as they could. What a commotion there was that morning! People shouting to one another, calling for help to haul in the fish that were swimming everywhere.

Yes, the old woman was also out but not with the other villagers. She was looking for fish in a quiet, secluded place on the beach. Not another person was in sight. With great difficulty she managed to catch a lot of fish. She didn't have the slightest idea what kind of fish they were.

The shells that she found were full of holes because of the sharp rocks. She checked inside each one carefully to see if perhaps a pearl was hidden inside. While looking for pearls she also chased after fish. What a busy morning, gathering shells, catching fish and putting them into her basket.

Suddenly she noticed a large pond with several big fish swimming in it. She rushed over in that direction and there caught a rock fish. It had a red mouth! The old woman was startled! In her surprise she said, "*Ah-ha*, maybe that rock fish stole my betel nut out of my basket, ate it, and now his lips are red!"

She was upset and thought for awhile. Then the old woman decided to go back to her house and check if the fish had indeed stolen the precious betel nut out of her bag.

During the walk back to the house, the old woman rested several times. She talked to some people who were fishing. However she never told a soul about the place where she had found the big rock fish. She feared if they knew they would certainly go and take all the fish.

When the old woman reached her house she stopped for a moment and took a deep breath. She opened the door, stepped inside and quickly went to the wall where her bag was hanging. Cautiously she peered inside. To her amazement there it was. The betel nut was there just as she had left it that morning.

"Maybe the rock fish ate his own betel nut and not mine," she said.

Even though the old woman was nearly exhausted, she suddenly remembered her fish in the pond on the beach. She hurried back as fast as her tired legs could go. But alas, the water had already risen, the tide had come in and taken all the fish back to sea. "How foolish I was to be so suspicious of the red-mouthed rock fish," she wailed. "Now I have no fish and must return home empty-handed and with a heavy heart."